I0631437

Edward Everett Hale

For fifty years; verses written on occasion, in the course of the

nineteenth century

Edward Everett Hale

For fifty years; verses written on occasion, in the course of the nineteenth century

ISBN/EAN: 9783743328273

Manufactured in Europe, USA, Canada, Australia, Japa

Cover: Foto ©ninafisch / pixelio.de

Manufactured and distributed by brebook publishing software
(www.brebook.com)

Edward Everett Hale

For fifty years; verses written on occasion, in the course of the nineteenth century

FOR FIFTY YEARS

VERSES WRITTEN ON OCCASION, IN THE COURSE OF THE NINETEENTH CENTURY

> " If it were his duty to write verses, he wrote verses; to fight slavers, he fought slavers; to write sermons, he wrote sermons; and he did one of these things with just as much alacrity as another." — *Memoir of Frederic Ingham*

BY

EDWARD E. HALE

AUTHOR OF "HOW TO DO IT," "TEN TIMES ONE IS TEN,"
"IN HIS NAME," AND "PRACTICAL CHRISTIANITY
APPLIED IN THE MANUFACTURE OF
WOOLLENS "

BOSTON

ROBERTS BROTHERS

1893

Copyright, 1895,
BY EDWARD EVERETT HALE.

University Press:
JOHN WILSON AND SON, CAMBRIDGE, U.S.A.

For such pleasure as these verses may give to my children and to theirs, and to some other friends, I have collected them, — with a certain difficulty, which will be easily understood.

To these indulgent readers they are dedicated.

EDWARD E. HALE.

Roxbury, April 13, 1893.

M41947

PREFACE.

THIS collection would hardly have been made but for the courage and kindness of the Ladies of my Staff. They were loyal enough to their chief to find these poems, to copy them, and to give me the collection in their own hand-writing, as a present on my birthday, — the day I was seventy years old.

When I saw that the collection was so considerable, I determined to print it, with the motto from Colonel Ingham's life, which I have copied on the titlepage. My children will be glad to have the book; let me hope that theirs will, as I know some unknown friends of mine will welcome it; for a book " is a letter to the friends we have never seen."

EDWARD E. HALE.

CONTENTS.

I. Ballads and History.

III. The War.

IV. Translations.

V. From Sermons and the Bible.

VI. Sonnets, Valentines, Birthdays, etc., and so forth.

I.

BALLADS AND HISTORY.

BALLADS AND HISTORY.

NEW ENGLAND'S CHEVY CHASE.

'TWAS the dead of the night. By the pine-
    knot's red light
  Brooks lay, half-asleep, when he heard the
    alarm, —
Only this, and no more, from a voice at the
    door:
  " The Red-Coats are out, and have passed
    Phips's farm."

Brooks was booted and spurred; he said never
    a word;
  Took his horn from its peg, and his gun from
    the rack;

To the cold midnight air he led out his white
    mare,
    Strapped the girths and the bridle, and sprang
        to her back.

Up the North Country Road at her full pace
        she strode,
    Till Brooks reined her up at John Tarbell's
        to say,
"We have got the alarm, — they have left
        Phips's farm;
    You rouse the East Precinct, and I 'll go this
        way."

John called his hired man, and they harnessed
        the span;
    They roused Abram Garfield, and Abram
        called me :
"Turn out right away; let no minute-man
        stay;
    The Red-Coats have landed at Phips's," says
        he.

By the Powder-House Green seven others fell in ;
  At Nahum's, the men from the Saw-Mill
    came down ;
So that when Jabez Bland gave the word of
  command,
  And said, " Forward, march!" there marched
    forward THE TOWN.

Parson Wilderspin stood by the side of the road,
  And he took off his hat, and he said, " Let us
    pray !
O Lord, God of Might, let thine angels of light
  Lead thy children to-night to the glories of
    day !
And let thy stars fight all the foes of the Right
As the stars fought of old against Sisera."

And from heaven's high arch those stars blessed
    our march,
  Till the last of them faded in twilight away ;
And with morning's bright beam, by the bank
    of the stream,
  Half the county marched in, and we heard
    Davis say :

"On the King's own highway I may travel all
      day,
   And no man hath warrant to stop me," says
      he;
"I've no man that's afraid, and I'll march at
      their head."
   Then he turned to the boys, — "Forward,
      march! Follow me."

And we marched as he said; and the Fifer he
      played
   The old "White Cockade," and he played
      it right well.
We saw Davis fall dead, but no man was afraid;
   That bridge we'd have had, though a thou-
      sand men fell.

This opened the play, and it lasted all day.
   We made Concord too hot for the Red-Coats
      to stay;
Down the Lexington way we stormed, black,
      white, and gray;
   We were first in the feast, and were last in
   •   the fray.

They would turn in dismay, as red wolves turn
    at bay.
  They levelled, they fired, they charged up
    the road.
Cephas Willard fell dead; he was shot in the
    head
  As he knelt by Aunt Prudence's well-sweep
    to load.

John Danforth was hit just in Lexington Street,
  John Bridge at that lane where you cross
    Beaver Falls,
And Winch and the Snows just above John
    Munroe's, —
  Swept away by one swoop of the big cannon-
    balls.

I took Bridge on my knee, but he said, "Don't
    mind me;
Fill your horn from mine, — let me lie where I be.
Our fathers," says he, "that their sons might
    be free,
Left their king on his throne, and came over
    the sea;

And that man is a knave or a fool who, to save
His life for a minute, would live like a slave."

Well, all would not do!   There were men good
        as new, —
    From Rumford, from Saugus, from towns far
        away, —
Who filled up quick and well for each soldier
        that fell;
    And we drove them, and drove them, and
        drove them, all day.
We knew, every one, it was War that begun,
When that morning's marching was only half
        done.

In the hazy twilight, at the coming of night,
    I crowded three buckshot and one bullet down.
'Twas my last charge of lead; and I aimed her
        and said,
    "Good luck to you, lobsters, in old Boston
        Town."

In a barn at Milk Row, Ephraim Bates and
        Monroe
    And Baker and Abram and I made a bed.

We had mighty sore feet, and we'd nothing
　　to eat;
　But we'd driven the Red-Coats, and Amos,
　　he said:
"It's the first time," says he, "that it's hap-
　　pened to me
　To march to the sea by this road where we've
　　come;
But confound this whole day, but we'd all of us
　　say
　We'd rather have spent it this way than to
　　home." *

The hunt had begun with the dawn of the sun,
　And night saw the wolf driven back to his den.
And never since then, in the memory of men,
　Has the Old Bay State seen such a hunting
　　again.

APRIL 19, 1882.

　* One of the veterans of the Lexington fight told
his story of it to Mr. Edward Everett. Mr. Everett
said, "You have never regretted that day, I am sure,"
and the old man replied, "Well, I'd rather have spent it
so than to hum."

THE GREAT HARVEST YEAR.*

THE night the century ebbed out, all worn
    with work and sin,
The night a twentieth century, all fresh with
    hope, came in,
The children watched, the evening long, the
    midnight clock to see,
And to wish to one another "A Happy Cen-
    tury!"
They climbed upon my knee, and they tumbled
    on the floor;
And Bob and Nell came begging me for stories
    of the War.

But I told Nell that I would tell no tales
    but tales of peace, —

* The harvest of the year 1878 was by far the largest
harvest which ever ripened in America. The exports
of food were much greater than ever before. They have
been much larger since.

God grant that for a hundred years the tales
    of war might cease!
I told them I would tell them of the blessed
    Harvest Store,
Of the year in which God fed men as they ne'er
    were fed before;
For till that year of matchless cheer, since suns
    or worlds were made,
Never sent land to other lands such gift of
    Daily Bread!

THE WAR was done, and men began to
    live in peaceful ways,
For thirteen years of hopes and fears, dark
    nights and joyful days.
If wealth would slip, if wit would trip, and
    neither would avail,
" Lo! the seed-time and the harvest," saith the
    Lord, " shall never fail."
And to all change of ups and downs, to every
    hope and fear,
To men's amaze came round the days of the
    Great Harvest Year,

When God's command bade all the land join
  heart and soul and mind,
And health and wealth, and hand and land, for
  feeding half mankind.

So hot the noons of ripe July that men took
  day for sleep,
And when the night shone clear and bright,
  they took their time to reap;
Nor can the men cut all the grain when hungry
  worlds are fed,
So the ready Ruths and Orpahs are gleaning
  in their stead.
All through the heated summer day the Kansas
  maidens slept,
All through the night, with laughter light, their
  moonlight vigil kept;
From set of sun the kindly moon until the
  break of day
Watched o'er their lightsome harvest-work, and
  cheered them on their way.
They drove their handsome horses down, they
  drove them up again,
While " click, click, click," the rattling knives
  cut off the heavy grain;

Before it falls, around the straw the waiting
  wires wind,
And the well-ordered sheaves are left in still
  array behind.
So laughing girls the harvest reap, all chattering
  the while,
While " click, click, click," the shears keep
  their chorus, mile by mile ;
And lazy Morning blushes when she sees the
  harvest stands
In ordered files, those miles on miles, to feed
  the hungry lands.*

Far in the South, from day to day, a living
  tide swept forth,
As, wave on wave, the herds of kine flowed
  slowly to the North.

---

* This verse was challenged, strange to say, by a
Western editor, who said Mr. Hale had drawn on his
imagination for his facts. I sent to one grange in
Kansas, offering a small present to any girl who would
give me her name as having driven a reaper by moonlight. I had to send four of my presents to kind
correspondents who had done so.

Great broad-horned oxen, tender-eyed, and such
        as Juno loved,
In troops no man could number, across the
        prairie moved.
Behind, along their wavy line, the brown ran-
        cheros rode,
From east to west, from west to east, as North
        the column flowed,
To keep the host compact and close from morn
        to setting sun,
Nor on the way leave one estray, as the great
        tide poured on.
A fair-haired Saxon boy beside commanded
        the array,
And as it flowed along the road, I heard the
        stripling say,
" 'T is God's command these beeves shall stand
        upon the Cheviot Hills,
The land to feed where rippling Tweed the
        lowland dews distils;"
So the great herd flows Northward, as the
        All-Father wills.

Far in the North the winter's gales blew
        sharply from northwest,
And locked the lakes and rivers, hard in their
        icy rest.

I saw men scrape the crystal lakes to clear them
    from the snow,
I saw them drive in long straight lines the
    ice-ploughs to and fro;
The blocks of amethyst they slid up to the
    sheltering shed
By the long lines of ready rail; and as they
    worked they said,
" Drive close the blocks, nor leave a chink
    between for breath of air;
Not winter's wind nor summer's sun may ever
    enter there,
But square and dry and hard and smooth the
    ice must ready be,
When summer suns are blazing, for its journey
    to the sea,
To pack the meat and keep it sweet, as the good
    God commands,
To feed his hungry children in so many waiting
    lands."

And far away from Northern ice and drifts of
    crystal snows,
On the rich coast where deep and red the
    Mississippi flows,

When the thick sugar-canes were ripe beneath
    the autumn sun
We listened for the earliest cock to tell of day
    begun.
In the cool sugar-house I slept upon my pallet
    bed,
Where Pierre Milhet, my princely host, had
    called his men, and said,
" At morning's call be ready all to meet here at
    the mill,
That not one drop may lazy stop before the vats
    we fill.
What man will be the first at dawn from lazy
    sleep to rise,
When the first gray of daybreak pales in the
    eastern skies,
What man will first his load of cane fling down
    before the door,
For that man's wife I give as prize this old-time
    louis d'or."
And all day long the hard-pressed mules the
    heaps of ripened cane
Brought swiftly to the mill, and then rushed
    back to bring again,

That all day long the rollers the fresh supply
    might grind,
Nor should one stalk be left not gleaned on the
    intervale behind.
So black and white, with main and might, are
    all united here,
Lest the harvest lack its sweets in God's Great
    Harvest Year.

The boys and girls the orchards thronged in
    those October days
Where the golden sun shone hotly down athwart
    the purple haze.
It warmed the piles of ruddy fruit which lay
    beneath the trees,
From which the apples, red and gold, fell down
    with every breeze.
The smallest boy would creep along to clasp
    the farthest bough,
And throw the highest pippin to some favored
    girl below.
The sound hard fruit with care we chose, we
    wiped them clean and dry,
While in the refuse heaps, unused, we let the
    others lie.

For pigs and cows and oxen those; for other
    lands were these,
And only what was hard and sound should sail
    across the seas.
Then, as the sun went down too soon, we piled
    the open crates,
And dragged them full where cellar cool threw
    wide its waiting gates,
So that the air which circled there was cold, but
    not too cold,
To keep for Eastern rivalry our Western fruit of
    gold.
And as old Evans thoughtful stood, and watched
    the boys that day,
I stood so near that I could hear the grim old
    Shaker say,
"Shame on our Yankee orchards, if the fruit
    should not be good,
The year the land at God's command sends
    half the world its food!"

I saw what wealth untold of corn our gracious
    God bestowed,
As for one autumn day I sped down the Rock
    River Road.

All night we slept; but still we kept our tireless
    way till morn,
And with the light, on left and right still
    stretched those shocks of corn.
A hundred thousand girls that year wore their
    engagement ring,
And a hundred thousand others before another
    spring;
But when the husking parties came, with all
    their frolic play,
Those " corn-fed maidens " might have kissed
    and kissed and kissed all day,
And although they kissed the boys but once for
    every thousandth ear,
They would not kiss for half the corn that
    blessed harvest year.
Yet buxom girls and hearty boys were ready, as
    they could,
To send love's blessing with the trains that took
    the world its food.
For since God smiled upon his child, in
    comfort or in care,
Was never yet such answer made to all his
    children's prayer.

A northeast gale, with snow and hail, bore
    down upon the sea;
With heavy rolls, beneath bare poles, we drifted
    to the lee.
When morning broke, the skipper spoke, and
    never sailor shirked,
But with a will, though cold and chill, from morn
    to night we worked.
Off in the spray the livelong day our spinning
    lines we threw,
And on each hook a struggling fish back to the
    deck we drew.
I know I looked to windward once, but the old
    man scowled, and said,
"Let no man flinch, nor give an inch, before
    his stent is made.
We've nothing for it, shipmates, but to heave
    the lines and pull,
Till each man's share has made the fare, and
    every cask is full.
This is no year for half a fare, for God this
    year decreed
That the forty States their hungry mates in all
    the lands shall feed."

No interval nor hind'rance the long procession
    break
Of the legion which the swine-herds drive by
    the City of the Lake.
Up death's long way it moves all day,
    unconscious of its fate,
As swine with boars contending hurry forward
    to the gate.
Thousands behind unwary crowd upon their
    leaders' tracks.
Nor hesitate nor falter as they near the
    headsman's axe.
For me, I stood away from blood and the silent
    stroke of death,
Where they packed the meat for the world to
    eat, in the basement crypt beneath.
I watched the task, as cask by cask was rolled
    by stalwart men,
And car on car to travel far was added to the
    train;
Nor ceased it then, but train on train pushed
    forth upon the rail,
Lest in some land the day's demand for daily
    food should fail.

For there shall not be a ship on the sea, to sail
    or far or near,
But the shipmates shall bless the plenteousness
    of the Great Harvest Year.

From last year's rice the black men the
    heaviest clusters choose,
And cull and thresh from every head the finest
    seed for use.
They beat it clean, they clayed it well, and
    when the field was sowed,
Up slid the sluice, and o'er the lands rushed in
    the waiting flood,
And then, without a ripple, above the trenches
    stood.
Soon through the glassy waters shot up the
    needles green,
With not a tare nor "volunteer" nor choking
    weed between.
Then month by month the joints grew up, so
    long and strong and high,
That the tall men who hoed them last were
    hidden from the sky.
But all the same, when harvest came, their
    sickles cut them low,

And they left the heads to ripen on the stubble
    patch below.
From field to flats, in flats to barns, they bear
    the rice, until
To thresh and beat, and clean and clear, they
    leave it at the mill.
The yellow husk is torn away, and the waiting
    casks receive
The stream of ice-white jewels from the great
    iron sieve.
So the black man's care sends out his share, for
    he knows that God has said
That his people here in his Harvest Year shall
    send his world its bread.

While fields were bright with summer light,
    and heaven was all ablaze,
O'er the broad Mohawk pastures I saw the cattle
    graze.
At early day they take their way, when cheerful
    morning warns,
And slowly leave the shelter of the hospitable
    barns.
The widow's son drew all the milk which the
    crowded bag would yield,

And sent his pretty Durham to her breakfast in
the field.
One portion then for the children's bowls the
urchin set away,
One part he set for cream for the next
churning-day;
But there was left enough for one little can
beside,
And with this the thrifty shaver to the great
cheese factory hied.
His milk was measured with the rest, and
poured into the stream,
And as he turned away he met Van Antwerp's
stately team,
Which bore a hundred gallons from the.
milking of that day,
And this was poured to swell the hoard fed by
that milky way.
The snowy curd is fitly stirred; the cruel
presses squeeze
Until the last weak drop has passed, and lo,
the solid cheese!
In Yorkshire mill, on Snowdon's hill, men eat it
with their bread,

Nor think nor ask of the distant task of the boy
    by whom they 're fed.
But when autumn 's done the widow's son stands
    at Van Antwerp's side,
And takes in his hand his dividend paid for the
    milky tide.

So South and North the food send forth to
    meet the nations' need;
So black and white, with main and might, the
    hungry peoples feed.
Since God bade man subdue the earth, and
    harvest-time began,
Never in any land has earth been so subdued
    by man.

———

PRAISE God for wheat, so white and sweet
    of which to make our bread!
Praise God for yellow corn, with which his
    waiting world is fed!
Praise God for fish and flesh and fowl, he gave
    to man for food!
Praise God for every creature which he made,
    and called it good!

Praise God for winter's store of ice! Praise
God for summer's heat!

Praise God for fruit-tree bearing seed; "to
you it is for meat"!

Praise God for all the bounty by which the
world is fed!

Praise God his children all, to whom he gives
their daily bread!

THE LAMENTABLE BALLAD OF THE BLOUDY BROOK.

As read at the Deerfield Celebration, October 17, 1888.

COME listen to the Story of brave Lathrop and
    his Men, —
How they fought, how they died,
When they marched against the Red Skins in
    the Autumn Days, and then
How they fell, in their pride,
By Pocumtuck Side.

"Who will go to Deerfield Meadows and bring
    the ripened Grain?"
Said old Mosely to his men in Array.
"Take the Wagons and the Horses, and bring it
    back again;
But be sure that no Man stray
All the Day, on the Way."

3

Then the Flower of Essex started, with Lathrop
    at their head,
    Wise and brave, bold and true.
He had fought the Pequots long ago, and now
    to Mosely said,
    " Be there Many, be there Few,
    I will bring the Grain to you."

They gathered all the Harvest, and marched
    back on their Way
    Through the Woods which blazed like
    Fire.
No Soldier left the Line of march to wander or
    to stray,
    Till the Wagons were stalled in the
    Mire,
    And the Beasts began to tire.

The Wagons have all forded the Brook as it
    flows,
    And then the Rear-Guard stays
To pick the Purple Grapes that are hanging from
    the Boughs,
    When, crack ! — to their Amaze,
    A hundred Fire-locks blaze !

Brave Lathrop, he lay dying; but as he fell he
    cried,
  "Each Man to his Tree," said he,
" Let no one yield an Inch; " and so the Soldier
    died;
  And not a Man of all can see
  Where the Foe can be.

And Philip and his Devils pour in their Shot
    so fast,
  From behind and before,
That Man after Man is shot down and breathes
    his last.
  Every Man lies dead in his Gore
  To fight no more, — no more!

Oh, weep, ye Maids of Essex, for the Lads who
    have died, —
  The Flower of Essex they!
The Bloody Brook still ripples by the black
    Mountain-side,
But never shall they come again to see the
    ocean-tide,
And never shall the Bridegroom return to his
    Bride,
  From that dark and cruel Day, — cruel Day!

THE BALLAD OF BEN FRANKLIN
AT THE INN. *

IT was Mr. Benjamin Franklin, a-carrying of
    the mail
    (Sing ho, for the tallow-chandler's brother!) ;
He had to be at Newport Friday morning
    without fail
    (Sing rather, t' other, pother, fuss, and
    bother!).
When passing Trustum Pond, as he rode with
    might and main,

---

* The historical authority for this ballad is in an
earlier excellent ballad, printed in the Connecticut Gaz-
ette in 1818. I wish I knew who wrote it. It was called
"Franklin's Wit," and begins, "Franklin, one night,
cold, freezing to his skin."

I am told that the story is more than two thousand
years old. The scene must have been between New
York and Newport, and I took the liberty to place it at
Willow Dell.

                          E. E. H.

He was soaked to the skin by the thunder and
the rain;
And when he came to Dead Man's Brook his
pony stumbled in,
And tumbled Mr. Franklin off, and wet him
through again
(Sing ho, for the tallow-chandler's mother!).

"Speed up," he cried, "and bring me to the inn
at Willow Dell"
(Sing ho, for the tallow-chandler's cousin!);
"Ben Seegar there shall give you oats and
Hiram groom you well"
(Sing ten, eleven, twelve, a baker's dozen!).
So quick they strode along the road, and here
he entered in,
And first, of course, he left his horse all wetted
to the skin.
But lo! so many people were around the
landlord's fire
That he was forced to stand outside, and
could n't come no nigher
(Sing five and four and two and one's a
dozen!).

" Good friend," said Mr. Franklin, as if it were
    of course
      (Sing Trustum Bay and lobster-claw and
      clam-shell !),
" I wish that you would give a peck of oysters
    to my horse "
      (Sing lobster-claw and pickerel and clam-
      shell !).
The landlord heard without a word; and quick
    as he was able,
He shelled the fish and took the dish of oysters
    to the stable;
And with surprise in all their eyes, the people
    left the stranger,
And crossed the yard in tempest hard, to crowd
    around the manger.
Ben Franklin, he cared not to see, but took the
    warmest seat,
And hung his coat above the fire, and sat and
    dried his feet
      (Sing centipede and crocodile and bomb-
      shell !).

Five minutes more, and through the door came
    Mr. Landlord, swearing
      (Sing Oliver, Tom Nopes, and Benjamin
      Seegar!);
And after him came all the folks, a-wondering
    and a-staring
      (Sing Oliver, Queen Moll, and Colonel
      Wager!).
"Your horse won't touch the oysters, sir,
    although they're fresh and new, sir."
"He won't?" asked Mr. Franklin; "That's no
    offence to you, sir.
You see he does n't know what's good; but if
    he don't, I do, sir"
      (Sing rheumatiz and gout and shaking
      ager!);
"If he had tried your oysters fried he might
    not then refuse 'em,
But I will sit and toast my feet while Mistress
    Bowers stews 'em."

ANNE HUTCHINSON'S EXILE.

A BALLAD.

"Home, home — where's my baby's home?
  Here we seek, there we seek my baby's home
    to find.
Come, come, come, my baby, come!
  We found her home, we lost her home, and
    home is far behind.
    Come, my baby, come!
    Find my baby's home!"

The baby clings; the mother sings; the pony
    stumbles on;
  The father leads the beast along the tangled,
    muddy way;
The boys and girls trail on behind; the sun will
    soon be gone,
  And starlight bright will take again the place
    of sunny day.

" Home, home — where 's my baby's home?
   Here we seek, there we seek, my baby's
      home to find.
Come, come, come, my baby, come!
   We found her home, we lost her home, and
      home is far behind.
     Come, my baby, come!
     Find my baby's home! "

The sun goes down behind the lake; the night
      fogs gather chill,
   The children's clothes are torn; and the
      children's feet are sore.
" Keep on, my boys, keep on, my girls, till all
      have passed the hill;
   Then ho, my girls, and ho, my boys, for fire
      and sleep once more! "
And all the time she sings to the baby on her
      breast,
" Home, my darling, sleep, my darling, find a
      place for rest;
Who gives the fox his burrow will give my bird
      a nest.
     Come, my baby, come!
     Find my baby's home! "

He lifts the mother from the beast; the hemlock
boughs they spread,
And make the baby's cradle sweet with fern-
leaves and with bays.
The baby and her mother are resting on their
bed;
He strikes the flint, he blows the spark, and
sets the twigs ablaze.
"Sleep, my child; sleep, my child!
Baby, find her rest,
Here beneath the gracious skies, upon her
father's breast;
Who gives the fox his burrow will give my
bird her nest.
Come, come, with her mother, come!
Home, home, find my baby's home!"

The guardian stars above the trees their loving
vigil keep;
The cricket sings her lullaby, the whippoorwill
his cheer.
The father knows his Father's arms are round
them as they sleep;
The mother knows that in His arms her
darling need not fear.

" Home, home, my baby's home is here ;
   With God we seek, with God we find the
      place for baby's rest.
Hist, my child, list, my child; angels guard us
      here.
   The God of heaven is here to make and keep
      my birdie's nest.
    Home, home, here 's my baby's home ! "

THE OLD SOUTH PICTURE-GALLERY.

[WRITTEN WHEN THE OLD SOUTH MEETING-HOUSE
OF BOSTON WAS DEDICATED TO PATRIOTISM AND
HISTORY.]

To hide the time-stains on our wall,
Let every tattered banner fall!
The Bourbon lilies, green and old,
That flaunted once in burnished gold;
The oriflamme of France that fell
That day when sunburned Pepperell
His shotted salvos fired so well,
The Fleur de Lys trailed sulky down,
And Louisburg was George's town.
The Bourbon yields it in despair
To Saxon arm and Pilgrim prayer.

Hang there the Lion and the Tower,
The trophies of an earlier hour,
Pale emblems of Castilian pride,
That shrouded Winslow when he died
Beneath Jamaica's palm.

Hang there, and there, the dusty rags
Which once were jaunty battle flags,
And for a week, in triumph vain,
Gay flaunted over blue Champlain,
Gayly had circled half the world,
Until they drooped, disgraced and furled,
That day the Hampshire line
Stood to its arms at dress parade,
Beneath the Stars and Stripes arrayed,
    And Massachusetts Pine,
To see the great atonement made
By Riedesel and Burgoyne.

Eagles which Caesar's hand had fed,
Banners which Charlemagne had led,
    A thousand years before,
A dozing empire meanly gave
To be the eagles of a slave,
And let the Hessian Landgrave wave
    Those banners on our shore.
The Hessian Landgrave basely sold
Eagle and flag for George's gold;
    And in the storm of war,
In crash of battle, thick and dark,
Beneath the rifle-shot of Stark,

The war-worn staff, the crest of gold,
The scutcheon proud and storied fold,
In surges of defeat were rolled.
So even Roman banners fall,
To screen the time-stains on our wall!

Beneath the war-flags' faded fold
I see our sovereigns of old
　　On magic canvas there.
The tired face of " baby Charles "
Looks sadly down from Pilgrim walls,
　　Half pride and half despair,
Doubtful to flatter or to strike,
　　To cozen or to dare.
His steel-clad charger he bestrides
As if to smite the Ironsides,
When Rupert with his squadron rides;
Yet such his gloomy brow and eye,
You wonder if he will not try
Once more the magic of a lie
　　To lift him from his care.

Hold still your truncheon! If it moves,
The ire of Cromwell's rage it braves!
　　For the next picture shows

The grim Protector on his steed,
Ready to pray, to strike, to lead, —
Dare all for England, which he saves,
New England, which he loves.

Vandyck drew Charles.   'T is Kneller there
Has pictured a more peaceful pair;
There Orange gives his last command,
The charter gives to Mather's hand;
And blooming there, the queenly she,
Who takes " now counsel, and now tea,"
Confounding Blenheim and Bohea,
Careless of war's alarm.

Yet as of old, the virgin Queen,
When armed for victory, might press
The smoky firelock of " Brown Bess,"
So Anna, in a fond caress,
Rests on a black " Queen's Arm."

Beneath those forms another band,
Silent but eloquent, shall stand.
There is no uttered voice nor speech
As still of liberty they teach;

No language and no sound is heard,
Yet still the everlasting word
Goes forth to thrill the land.
Story and Greenough shall compel
The silent marble forms to tell
The lesson that they told so well,
      Lesson of Fate and Awe, —
Franklin still point the common place
      Of Liberty and Law;
Adams shall look in Otis' face,
Blazing with Freedom's soul;
And Molyneux see Hancock trace
The fatal word which frees a race,
There, in New England's well-earned place,
      The head of Freedom's roll.

These are not all.   The past is gone,
But other victories shall be won,
For which the time-worn tale we read
Is but the sowing of the seed.
The harvest shall be gathered when
Our children's children meet again
      Upon this time-worn floor;
When ruddy drops flush living cheek,
And tribunes of the people speak

As living man can speak to living men;
When future Adamses conspire,
When other Danas feed the fire,
Each grandson worthy of his sire;
When other Phillipses shall tell
Again the tale he tells so well;
When other Minots shall record
The victories of some other Ward,
And other Prescotts tell the story
Of other Warrens' death and glory;
When, in some crisis of the land,
Some other Quincy takes the stand,
To teach, to quicken, to command, —
          To speak with prophet's power
Of Liberty and Law combined,
Of Justice close with Mercy joined,
United in one heart and mind;
That talisman of victory find
In which our laurels all are twined, —
          And for one struggle more
Forget those things which lie behind,
          And reach to those before.

4

THE THREE ANNIVERSARIES.

SHORT is the day, and night is long;
    But he who waits for day
In darkness sits not quite so long,
    And earlier hails the twilight gray, —
A little earlier hails the ray
That drives the mists of night away.

So was this land cold, dead, and drear,
    When to the rock-bound shore
That Pilgrim band, Christ-led, drew near,
The promise of a new-born year, —
Twilight, which shows that even here
The sun of gladness shall appear,
The land be dark no more.

So was the world dark, drear, and wild,
    When on that blessed morn
A baby on his mother smiled.
The dawning comes, the royal child,
    The Sun of life, is born.

The lengthening days shall longer grow,
 Till summer rules the land ;
From Pilgrim rills full rivers flow, —
 Roll stronger and more grand.
So, Father, grant that year by year
The Sun of Righteousness more clear
To our awaiting hearts appear,
And from his doubtful East arise
The noonday Monarch of the skies, —
Till darkness from the nations flies ;
Till all know him as they are known,
Till all the earth be all his own.

DECEMBER 25, 1847.

THE STORY OF A DORY.

IF you will look into my garden
Some autumn, you 'll find your reward in
The sight of a flower-decked dory,
Of which I will now tell the story.

This dory was built on the plan
Approved by a sea-faring man;
She was built on the shore of Cape Ann.

At first she was painted dark green,
And indeed was the finest machine
Of her species that ever was seen.

Her qualities first were essayed in
A voyage she made for Menhaden,
From which she returned deeply laden.

There were bushels on bushels galore;
And the people who stood on the shore
Declared they had never seen more.

One time she was out with Luke Foster,
So long that the people of Gloucester
Were sure that the dory was lost, or
At least would be seen there no more.

But the dory was really all right,
And appeared full of fish before night.
The people rejoiced at the sight,
And praised her as never before.

You should see how Dan Ober set sail,
Before a sou-sou-western gale,
And never he needed a pail,
For there was not a spoonful to bail.

So well did the dory behave,
And so lightly spring over the wave,
That if Ober's lips were not mute, he
Would say that this vision of beauty
Exulted in doing her duty.

Dan Foster the business plied,
And always brought home to his bride
A boatful of fish on each tide.

Dan Foster's twin brother, he cried
Fresh haddock and cod far and wide;
The neighborhood all were supplied,
And the country on every side.

And now is the story all told,
For the dory which once was so bold
Grew timorous as she grew old.

She lay in a faint on the shore,
Did not go to sea as before,
And grew dry and leaked more and more.

And forgetting the scenes she had been to,
When Dan Foster had died, as all men do,
The dory was sold at a vendue.

The people who sold her, with powers
From Dan Foster's will, made her ours;
And now, every autumn of showers,
This oldest of dories embowers
With semi-tropical flowers.

The colors are scarlet and gory,
But peaceful, for all that, the story,
Of this autumn decline of the dory,
Which floats all its banners of glory.

THE BALLAD OF THE BELL.

THREE gallant knights ride down the road, —
  They use nor spur nor rein;
In laugh and jest they little bode
That on this way their steeds have trod
  They turn not back again.

They laugh and chat along the way,
  These noble lords of Spain, —
No haste to go, no care to stay,
A dusty road, a sunny day;
And little heed the three that they
  Will ne'er go back again.

" Groom, take this horse; Boy, feed him well!"
  Ah, me, a caution vain!
Yet not one warning voice to tell
How ends this Council of the Bell,
How each man falls beneath the spell,
  And goes not back again!

A flashing axe, a headsman's sword,
   Three falling trunks, and then,
With never prayer or shriving word,
Lies stark in death each laughing lord,
   And none goes back again.

HUESCA, ARRAGON,
   June, 1882.

II.

COLLEGE VERSES.

COLLEGE VERSES.

FROM "CLASS POEM," 1839.

If they scribble in ballads, their young
    Lochinvar
Shall boast of no steed but his steam-rushing
    car, —
Save his high pressure engine, companions have
    none,
As he rides all unarmed, as he rides all alone.
And though no such change will e'er come
    upon love,
Which is fixed upon bases which never can move;
Though it flow like the Solway, and ebb like its
    tide,
As it has through all ages, since Eve was a
    bride ;
Though one touch to the hand and one word
    in the ear
Shall ever be proof an elopement is near, —

To what a strange seat his fair lady he 'll swing!
How quick to the safety-valve after her spring!
And his cry, " She is won, and no turnpike can
    bar;
They 've good boilers that follow the young
    Lochinvar."

Heaven shield them from trying, as thus they
    rush on,
To swim the Eske river, where ford there is
    none;
Though matchless we own them for swift
    locomoting,
These iron-built horses are not fit for floating.
Yet the poet might hint 't was in Eske's surges
    drowned,
Why fair Ellen of Netherby never was found;
And if for dénouement more sad he were
    faulted,
Let his boiler collapse, and his lovers be
    scalded.

[There is no reason for printing these lines, but that they mark the curiosity which belonged to the locomotive for many years after the success of the "Rocket," in 1829.]

A SONG FOR THE PHI BETA KAPPA DINNER OF 1839.

(To be sung to "Jessie of Dumblane.")

WHEN green-eyed Minerva asked Paris to serve
    her,
    And give her the apple gift offered by
      Strife,
All other gifts scorning, she gave him a warning,
    And bade him make wisdom his pilot thro'
      life.

But the little god Cupid this lesson thought stupid,
    And so he convinced the unfortunate boy;
He sought after pleasure, — refused her the
      treasure;
    And that shake of his head was the ruin of
      Troy.

Some hundred years after this fatal disaster
    The Greek Epicurus established his fame;
He showed what a blunder poor Paris was under,
    For wisdom and pleasure were one and the
      same.

And even in this time we think pleasure wisdom,
    Whatever the Alford Professor may say;
We 'll applaud him next week if he " rows up the
        Greek,"
    But we own ourselves Epicureans to-day.

With old friends beside us, let old wisdom
        guide us, —
    Let pleasure be wisdom, at least for a day;
With this κυβερνήτης our band of Phi Beta's
    Will once in a twelvemonth laugh sorrow
        away.

1864.

I.

SHALL the first strain upon the lyre unused
        Speak as of old,
        When oft it told
        Of blush and sigh,
        Of hope and fear
        And smile and tear,
Of those most beautiful in boyhood's eye?
Shall it sing her, the queen of camps and groves,
        Sing of our loves?
        So let it sing again;
        Surely as men,
        In the refrain
        Of that eternal strain,
We can sound chords of which we knew not
        then!

II.

Or shall the new string on the rusty lyre
      Weep with our woes, —
Speak *in memoriam* of our loved and lost,
Of bleeding steps of life and what they cost,
Of wreaths that crumbled when we prized them
      most —
Of yawning gulfs where sunk our tempest-tost?
      Such songs as those
      In minor strain
      We can attune as men
With such a wail of hearts that feel real woes
As Byron school-boys' anguish never knows!

III.

Or shall we sing of Hope, — of kingdoms yet
      to win,
Of worlds released from pain and saved from sin,
      Of good times come again?
That vision seen beneath the rainbow arch,
Of blessed futures in their Godward march,
      We see as men
      As never then.

That vision brightens, and that future glows ;
Who knows his failures, — what he hopes for
knows !

IV.

Does Memory sing?
Some silver wedding bid the bard rehearse, —
Life's lengthening legend in his lengthening
verse ;
Call on Mnemosyne soft-tongued
To tell the tale each day prolonged, —
With all her drowsy grace
Its picture growing dim to trace.
Is that the song inspires
Our new awakened lyres?
We men can sing — as never years ago !
We men have something to remember now !

V.

Seven-stringed our lyre ; it beat with love of old,
With love beats now !
Grief, hope and victory, too, — their tale it told ;
It tells it now !

5

Of brooding memory the song it sings,
For patriot war the bloody laurel brings,
      Nor lacks the while
      This joyous smile
      Of happy home,
      Past — and to come.
Such chords, new tuned, we strike as men, —
Chords better tuned and better struck than then.

VI.

      And if our poet rise
      To the one theme which tries
      All high emprise
      Beneath — beyond the skies, —
If to his Lyre he add the octave chord,
Which chimes with each to sing the Eternal
      Word
And sound the praise of the Eternal God, —
      With every year
      That comes and goes,
      With every tear
      That fills and flows,
He knows that God as never known before ;
As he floats nearer to the Eternal shore

His love he sings, and scans his purpose, too,
With joy the prating schoolboy never knew.

VII.

Aye as we live, Life's song is better sung,
Aye as we live, Life's lyre more tuneful strung, —
The blind receive their sight, the dumb their
   tongue.
Aye as he grows, God's child becomes more
   young!

ALMA MATER'S ROLL.

AT THE PHI BETA KAPPA DINNER OF 1875.*

I SAW her scan her sacred scroll,—
I saw her read her record roll
Of men who wrought to win the right,
Of men who fought and died in fight;
When now a hundred years by-gone
The day she welcomed Washington,
She showed to him her boys and men,
And told him of their duty then.

" Here are the beardless boys I sent,
And whispered to them my intent
To free a struggling continent.

" The marks upon this scroll will show
Their words a hundred years ago.

* Many of the gentlemen named in the last verse but
one were present at the dinner.

" Otis ! " " No lesser death was given
To him than by a bolt from heaven ! "
" Quincy ! " " He died before he heard
The echo of his thunder word."
" And these were stripling lads whom I
Sent out to speak a nation's cry,
In ' glittering generality '
Of living words that cannot die :

" John Hancock ! " " Here." " John Adams ! "
        " Here."
" Paine, Gerry, Hooper, Williams ! " " Here."
" My Narragansett Ellery ! " " Here."
" Sam Adams, first of freemen ! " " Here."
" My beardless boys, my graybeard men,
Summoned to take the fatal pen
Which gave eternal rights to men, —
  All present, or accounted for."

I saw her scan again the scroll, —
I heard her read again the roll ;
I heard her name her soldier son,
Ward, called from home by Lexington.
He smiled and laid his baton down,
Proud to be next to Washington !

He called her list of boys and men
Who served her for her battles then.
From North to South, from East to West,
He named her bravest and her best,
From distant fort, from bivouac near:
"Brooks, Eustis, Cobb, and Thacher!" "Here."
Name after name, with quick reply,
As twitched his lip and flashed his eye;
But then he choked and bowed his head, —
"Warren at Bunker Hill lies dead."

The roll was closed; he only said,
  "All present, or accounted for."

That scroll is stained with time and dust;
They were not faithless to their trust.
"If those days come again, — if I
Call on the grandsons, — what reply?
What deed of courage new display
These fresher parchments of to-day?"

I saw her take the newer scroll, —
I heard her read the whiter roll;
And as the answers came, the while
Our mother nodded with a smile:

"Charles Adams!" "Here." "George Ban-
croft!" "Here."
"The Hoars!" "Both here." "Dick Dana!"
"Here."
"Wadsworth!" "He died at duty's call."
"Webster!" "He fell as brave men fall."
"Everett!" "Struck down in Faneuil Hall."
"Sumner!" "A nation bears his pall."
"Shaw, Abbott, Lowell, Savage!" "All
Died there, — to live on yonder wall!"
"Come East, come West, come far, come near,—
Lee, Bartlett, Davis, Devens!" "Here."
"All present, or accounted for."

Boys, heed the omen! Let the scroll
Fill as it may as years unroll;
But when again she calls her youth
To serve her in the ranks of Truth,
May she find all one heart, one soul, —
At home or on some distant shore,
"All present, or accounted for!"

HARVARD AND YALE.

At an Alpha Delta Dinner at Middletown,
Connecticut, May, 1878.

When Harvard woke in woodland wild,
Our dear New England's first-born child
    (Before her she had nary one),
The damsel tried to break away;
Indeed she proved a little gay,
    Or Latitudinarian.

The dear old mother did not grout;
    She never thought to scold or spite her;
The only thing she cared about
Was that when sister Yale came out,
    She should be laced a little tighter.

The girls themselves no difference knew, —
    They laughed and joked, and quarrelled
      never.
As loving sisters both they grew;
And with each year's Commencement new,
They twine the crimson with the blue,
    Kiss and make friends, and will forever.

FOR FORTY YEARS.

At the Alpha Delta Phi Convention, May 8, 1879.

For Forty Years
Of mingled hopes and fears,—
Of tales of battle, told with bated breath,
Of peace, returning with her olive wreath,
Of love, of joy, of sorrow, and of death!

For suns will sink, and twilights melt away,
Cool evenings hurry on, nor midnight stay,
But at the summons of the morn e'en night
       grows gray,
Stars fade from sight, and lo, the light, the day!

Such change from day to night,
From dark to light,
Fills up the record of my forty years.

For Forty Years
You boys look forward on another page.

The hall is dressed; the candles are not lit;
The page is white, — the annals are not writ;
The stage is set, the curtain pulled away,
The actors dressed and ready for the play,
And I for chorus stand ;
                              Is it for me
To say if it be farce or tragedy?
What shall the dancers dance, or what the rage
That heaves the history of the stormy age,
        For Forty Years?

Not mine !   For Forty Years
The stage is all your own ; the page is yours,
        Of storm or peace,
        Of work or ease,
Of winter tempests or of summer showers;
        Not mine to tell
What hand shall work for woe, or what work
        well !

        Only this oracle for gathering strife,
        Only this lesson from a happy life ;

Who lives and works for Love
The miracle shall prove;

The Eternal Power is his, whate'er he do;
Weakness is strength for him, and old things
      are made new,
As he mounts higher on these rounds of time,
His grasp more sure, his foot more quick to
      climb.

    Faster the race is run,
    As one by one
Our selfish handicaps away we fling.
    Love works the miracle of youth, —
    Love speaks the oracle of truth;
    And they who prove
    The strength of love
Grow younger and more young
    For Forty Years!

THE CALL TO DINNER.

AT THE PHI BETA KAPPA MEETING OF 1884, — AFTER
MR. BAYARD'S ADDRESS.

[There was no poet. I was presiding, and invited the assembly to
dinner in these words.]

WHEN Nestor ended, 'mid the loud acclaim,
As echoing plaudits sounded down the shore,
If from the listening ranks some stripling came,
And like some Oliver, demanded more,
The graver chieftains of maturer age
Half heard and half deferred his bold request;
They bade each beardless youth, each hoary
        sage,
Wait for the sequel till they 'd done the feast.

For down the shore, by smoke and vapor hid,
The cooks were basting while the spits went
        round,
With savory porker or with savory kid,
While bubbling gravy wasted on the ground.

Phi Beta follows in this classic way,
Postpones the sequel of the charmed discourse,
At groaning tables breaks the passing day,
And mingles wisdom with the second course.

For gamesome kid, we roast the summer lamb ;
For heating wines we drink the cooling ice ;
Recall their boar's meat in our savory ham ;
Then quicken memories, and exchange advice,—
Tell the old stories of forgotten fields,
And try the fortunes which the future yields.

To rites like these, brethren, assemble all,—
Leaving these seats, repair to yonder hall,
And form procession at the marshal's call.

AT COMMENCEMENT DINNER,

JULY, 1889.

IT is not day, and yet the night is gone.
   Look eastward, — see! that is not black,
     but gray, —
Cold gray, hard gray, dark gray; and yet if one
   Watches it, cold and hard, he hopes for day.
Whiter and whiter, — see, the night is done!
   The stars are frightened, and they pale
     away.
Color that —   Color? Yes, 'neath Procyon.
See the soft tinge, as new as it is old,
That nameless yellow of which Homer told,
And then, as those weird curtains are unrolled,
Cloud mixed with cloud, fold tangled in with
     fold,
That "faint, peculiar tint of yellow green,"
And there, the scarlet of the rays between, —
Scarlet — no, crimson, flashing into gold,
One sea of gold, and then the Sun! the Sun!

III.

THE WAR.

THE WAR.

———•———

TAKE THE LOAN.

COME, freemen of the land,
Come meet the great demand,
True heart and open hand, —
    Take the loan!
For the hopes the prophets saw,
For the swords your brothers draw,
For liberty and law,
    Take the loan!

Ye ladies of the land,
As ye love the gallant band
Who have drawn a soldier's brand,
    Take the loan!
Who would bring them what she could,
Who would give the soldier food,
Who would staunch her brothers' blood,
    Take the loan!

All who saw our hosts pass by,
All who joined the parting cry,
When we bade them do or die,
 Take the loan !
As ye wished their triumph then,
As ye hope to meet again,
And to meet their gaze like men,
 Take the loan !

Who would press the great appeal
Of our ranks of serried steel,
Put your shoulders to the wheel, ·
 Take the loan !
That our prayers in truth may rise,
Which we press with streaming eyes
On the Lord of earth and skies,
 Take the loan !

MAY, 1861.

OLD FANEUIL HALL.

COME, soldiers, join a Yankee song,
And cheer us, as we march along,
With Yankee voices, full and strong,—
    Join in chorus all;
Our Yankee notions here we bring,
Our Yankee chorus here we sing,
To make the Dixie forest ring
    With OLD FANEUIL HALL!

When first our fathers made us free,
When old King George first taxed the tea,
They swore they would not bend the knee,
    But armed them one and all!
In days like those the chosen spot
To keep the hissing water hot,
To steep the tea leaves in the pot,
    Was OLD FANEUIL HALL!

So when, to steal our tea and toast,
At Sumter first the rebel host

Prepared to march along the coast,
    At Jeff Davis' call,
He stood on Sumter's tattered flag,
To cheer them with the game of brag,
And bade them fly his Rebel Rag
    On OLD FANEUIL HALL!

But war's a game that two can play;
They waked us up that very day,
And bade the Yankees come away
    Down South, at Abram's call!
And so I learned my facings right,
And so I packed my knapsack tight,
And then I spent the parting night
    In OLD FANEUIL HALL!

And on that day which draws so nigh,
When rebel ranks our steel shall try, —
When sounds at last the closing cry
    " Charge bayonets all ! "
The Yankee shouts from far and near,
Which broken ranks in flying hear,
Shall be a rousing Northern cheer
    From OLD FANEUIL HALL!

1862.

PUT IT THROUGH!

Come, Freemen of the land,
Come, meet the last demand, —
Here's a piece of work in hand;
    Put it through!
Here's a log across the way,
We have stumbled on all day;
Here's a ploughshare in the clay, —
    Put it through!

Here's a country that's half free,
And it waits for you and me
To say what its fate shall be;
    Put it through!
While one traitor thought remains,
While one spot its banner stains,
One link of all its chains, —
    Put it through!

Hear our brothers in the field,
Steel your swords as theirs are steeled,
Learn to wield the arms they wield, —
    Put it through!
Lock the shop and lock the store,
And chalk this upon the door, —
" We 've enlisted for the war!"
    Put it through!

For the birthrights yet unsold,
For the history yet untold,
For the future yet unrolled,
    Put it through!
Lest our children point with shame
On the fathers' dastard fame,
Who gave up a nation's name,
    Put it through!

1864.

THE INTERNAL REVENUE.

[A New Version of an Old Song.]

WHEN Abraham spends without measure,
　　Sending armies and navies afar,
Who fills up the chests of his treasure,
　　Who tightens the sinews of war?
Undaunted by danger or omen,
　　'Tis the In-ter-nal Revenue,
That flaunts in the face of the foeman
　　　　The flag of the Red, White, and Blue.

Each stamp breaks a link of our fetters,
　　Breaks chains that were tight round our necks,
Hurrah for the red on our letters!
　　Hurrah for the blue on our checks!
Like the crimson blood of our bravest,
　　Who are tracking the snow wastes through,
Like the foam on the sea of our navies,
Hurrah for the Red, White, and Blue!

　　1864.

IV.

TRANSLATIONS.

TRANSLATIONS.

A CHORUS FROM IPHEGENIA IN TAURIS.

STROPHE.

HALCYON, O Halcyon,
Who by Pontus' rocky shore
Singest mournful evermore,
  In a song whose tones are clear
  If kindred sorrow lends an ear,
Calling for thy husband lost,
  Brooding on the sea, —
Wingless halcyon of the foam,
  I can grieve with thee.
Grieving for the home I love,
  Longing for Diana's shrine,
Where she dwells in Cynthian grove,
Where purple fold and locks of gold
  Deck her form divine;

For the fragrant Daphne's flowers;
   For the olive's fruitage sere,
   Precious gift of loved Latona,
   Mother of our goddess dear;
   For the consecrated lake,
   Where their thirst her cygnets slake,
   And their refuge joyful take
   And their pæan worship make,
Where the green shore's glad echoes ring,
While to the Muses these melodious sing.

ANTISTROPHE.

Oh, the tears, the streams of tears
   Which in sorrow-torrents fell
When they forced me from my home,
   I shall aye remember well, —
When the precious price was paid,
When the oars in ocean played,
And hostile barks the captives bore
Seaward to this barbarous shore,
   Where we serve Atrides' child,
   Sad priestess, who has never smiled
   In this altar-worship wild.

For habit does not teach us
In our sorrows to be glad;
Their misery will reach us
Through what time our lives we lead.
This heavy fate of man shall never end, —
Grief with his pleasure evermore shall blend.

STROPHE II.

For you, our honored mistress,
Shall the Argive's fifty oars
Struggle with the surge of ocean
Till you see your native shores.
They shall flash and flash again,
To the merry notes of Pan,
While softer tones of Phœbus' lyre
Shall hasten to an end
The weary days which bring your bark
To Attic strand.
I linger here deserted, — woe is me,
But you shall cross the madly surging sea.
The halyards high your sails in sky
Broad display,
And your ship before the tempest's roar
Flies away.

ANTISTROPHE II.

Oh that through the ethereal course,
Where the sun his radiance pours,
I might hasten to those shores!
Oh that, wing-borne o'er the foam,
I might fly to my home!
I would sing in chorus there
Where the virgin goddess fair,
Of happy birth,
Welcomes throngs who eager press,
With the prayer that she may bless
Them on the earth,
Where at the sacred shrine
Of Locks of Gold,
Her suitors vie with gifts divine,
Rivals bold,
That her smiles may bless the prayer
Which in reverence they bear
To Latona, mother dear;
With apparel rich and rare
Her downy cheek and golden hair
They enfold.

1843.

FROM HEINE.

MIDNIGHT rests upon the city
  Through whose shaded streets I go;
An hour ago all smiled or sorrowed;
  The hour is past, — they 're dreaming now.
    Pleasure like a flower has faded;
      Drained the wine-cup's sparkling stream;
    Grief's fires, like the sun, are shaded,
      That the weary world may dream.
        Let it dream, then!
        Let it dream!

All my haste and all my anger,
  Shivering, broken, fly away,
As I see the moon in slumber,
  Resting from her strife with day.
    Light as whispers, soft as starlight,
      Through all space my spirit goes, —
    Light as sound and still as starlight
      Visits men in their repose,
        In the secrets
          Of their dreams.

Here a palace stands before me;
Ha! its dreamer flies abroad!
Craven, careworn, and remorse-worn,
See him, trembling, seek his sword!
Hist! In flight a thousand coursers
Bear him from his throne away, —
Ha! He falls on earth, and yawning
She engulfs him as her prey!
God of vengeance,
Let him dream!

Everywhere the spirit enters:
Ope we here the prison door, —
Germany, thy sons are fettered
For the love of thee they bore!
Here the captive sleeps forgetful;
Does he dream of freedom now?
Does he dream of battles over,
Victory's garland on his brow?
God of Freedom,
Let him dream!

Yet a step, and here the cabin
Of the tiller of the soil.
To his slumber God has given
Dreams which pay for daylight's toil.

Every seed which Morpheus scatters
  Gives a golden harvest birth, —
Fills the dreamer's little cottage
  With the treasures of the earth.
    God, who carest for the poor man,
      Let him dream!

Here I pause to speak my blessing!
  Dearest, who art life to me,
You are not my only loved one, —
  Freedom shares my heart with thee!
    While the stainless doves of promise
      To your cradle blessings bore,
    Round me in my baby slumbers
      Pranced mad coursers wild for war.
    While I dream of Freedom's eagles,
      Of the bold, unflinching eye,
    Dearest, in more peaceful slumbers
      You shall watch the butterfly.
        God of love,
          Oh, let her dream!

1843.

7

NEPTUNE DESCENDING.

THERE he sat high, retired from the seas;
There looked with pity on his Grecians beaten;
There burned with rage at the god-king who
slew them.
Then he rushed forward from the rugged moun-
tains,
Quickly descending;
He bent the forests also as he came down,
And the high cliffs shook under his feet.
Three times he trod upon them,
And with his fourth step reached the home he
sought for.

There was his palace, in the deep waters of the
seas,
Shining with gold, and builded forever.
There he yoked him his swift-footed horses;
Their hoofs are brazen, and their manes are
golden.

He binds them with golden thongs,
He seizes his golden goad,
He mounts upon his chariot and doth fly, —
Yes! he drives them forth into the waves!
And the whales rise under him from the depths,
For they know he is their king;
And the glad sea is divided into parts,
That his steeds may fly along quickly;
And his brazen axle passes dry between the
    waves.

So, bounding fast, they bring him to his
    Grecians.

FROM MARTIAL.

COME and see our Spaniards, Lician, —
    Other lands shall never shame us;
Come, and see my Bilbilis,
    Both for arms and horses famous.
Come to craggy Vadavero;
    Come, and rest you in the groves
Of my dainty, sweet Botrodes,
    Which the blithe Pomona loves.
You shall bathe in warm Congedus,
    Which the water-nymphs environ,
Or in freezing Salo cool you,
    Where we cool our blades of iron.
Beasts and birds shall make your dinner,
    As you cross Vobisca's meadows;
Golden Tagus shall refresh you,
    Underneath her leafy shadows.

Are you thirsty? Here 's Dircenna,
   And Nemea's melted snows;
Or when fierce December rages,
   And the Gallic north-wind blows,
We 'll go down to Tarragona,
   To Laletania repair, —
You shall shoot the does with arrows,
   You shall shoot the wild boar there ;
The keeper shall bring home the stag,
   And you, on horseback, course the hare.

Far away be squabbling clients,
   Far away Liburnus, too ;
Not a dun shall break your slumbers, —
   You shall sleep the morning through.
You shall hear no woman whimper,
   And no senator debate ;
Other men to bores shall listen,
   Others hear the fools dilate.
You know how to taste the pleasure
   When your Sura wins his meed ;
We know how to keep the treasure, —
   How to live, and live indeed.

UNIV. OF
CALIFORNIA

V.

FROM SERMONS AND THE BIBLE.

[I took from Dr. Doddridge the hint of putting together in verses, at the end of a sermon, whatever there was to say.

I have observed, in his case, that the verses are remembered, while the sermons are forgotten. " Therefore speak I unto them in parables."   E. E. H.]

FROM SERMONS, ETC.

ALL SOULS.

WHAT was his name?   I do not know his
    name.
I only know he heard God's voice and came;
  Brought all he loved across the sea,
  To live and work for God — and me;
    Felled the ungracious oak,
      With horrid toil
      Dragged from the soil
   The thrice-gnarled roots and stubborn
    rock;
With plenty filled the haggard mountain-side,
And when his work was done, without
    memorial died.
No blaring trumpet sounded out his fame;
He lived, he died.   I do not know his name.

No form of bronze and no memorial stones
Show me the place where lie his mouldering
    bones.

Only a cheerful city stands,
Builded by his hardened hands;
Only ten thousand homes,
Where every day
The cheerful play
Of love and hope and courage comes;
These are his monuments, and these alone, —
There is no form of bronze and no memorial
stone.

And I?
Is there some desert or some boundless sea
Where thou, great God of angels, wilt send me?
Some oak for me to rend, some sod
For me to break,
Some handful of thy corn to take,
And scatter far afield,
Till it in turn shall yield
Its hundredfold
Of grains of gold,
To feed the happy children of my God? —
Show me the desert, Father, or the sea.
Is it thine enterprise? Great God, send me!
And though this body lie where ocean rolls,
Father, count me among all faithful souls!

"IN LOVE THE LIFE OF HEAVEN
WE FOUND."

I WENT to learned men and asked the way.
The learned men were lost among their books;
They bade me stand aside, for such as they
For such as me had neither words nor looks.

I went to churches, where beyond my sight
Priests and their servants served great mystery;
Their waves of incense filled the arches' height,
Their waves of music swelled in harmony.
But I stood all alone: and he and he
Who led the great procession had no care for
     me.

I left their church, and sought the street instead,
To find a cripple crouched upon the ground.
I took him to my home and called for aid,
From palace and from hovel, all around.
His wounds we tended and his hunger fed, —
And lo! in love the life of heaven we found.

UNDER LAURELS AND MAPLES.

A THOUSAND sounds, and each a joyful sound:
The dragon-flies are darting as they please;
The humming-birds are humming all around;
The clethra all alive with buzzing bees.
Each playful leaf its separate whisper found,
As laughing winds went rustling through the
        grove;
And I saw thousands of such sights as these,
And heard a thousand sounds of joy and love.

And yet so dull I was, I did not know
That He was there who all this love displayed;
I did not think how He who loved us so
Shared all my joy, — was glad that I was glad;
And all because I did not hear the word
In English accents say, " It is the Lord."

THE CARAVAN.

In the rough chapparal I slept alone, —
No roof above me, and the stones my bed.
Alone I waked; no man had heard my groan,
No whisper cheered me, and no guide had led.
I wandered right and left away from man,
And when the day was done, I was where I
     began.

One morn I wakened to the cheer of song
Of a great caravan which camped hard by;
Shyly I joined the gay and happy throng,
Which gladly took me in their company.
They fed my hunger, and my wounds they
     bound;
I went with them, and Home and Heaven were
     found.

JEHOVAH LIVETH.

*And though they say, The Lord liveth, surely they swear
falsely.* — *Jeremiah* v. 2.

PRIESTS offer Sheba's incense and sweet cane,
  Responding, each to each, "*Jehovah lives !*"
His car through death the maddened warrior
    drives,
Raising the cry, "*Jehovah lives!*" again;
The watchmen at the gate their guard maintain,
  "*Jehovah lives !*" the countersign each gives.
  "*Jehovah lives!*" the monarch cries, and
    strives
With such a spell his sceptre to sustain!
  Yet altar priests a hireling service give,
And crimsoned warriors fight for fame and gold,
  The guards with tales of peace their lords
    deceive,
Whose tyrant hands a blood-stained sceptre hold.
Why with such lies the Lord of Nations
    grieve?
In your false hearts Jehovah does not live!

THE LORD OF THE VINEYARD.

WHO came at the eleventh hour,
    And to their tasks were true,
And labored each as he had power,
    Received — each man his due.

Who came when day was breaking bright,
    And labored all day through,
Till evening melted into night,
    Received — each man his due.

These looked at those, those looked at these,
    As from their Lord they came;
The dues of those, the dues of these,
    They saw, were just the same.

For those and these God's children are,
    Born for eternity;
Moments of time could not compare
    With lives which live for aye.
And souls whose every hope is fixed above
Have no less due from God than all a
    Father's love.

"AS A LITTLE CHILD."

"Thou must be born again!" O thou whose
    voice
  In thunder tones would visit all the earth,
  In lightning words would preach this heavenly
    birth,
So men may weep where most they should
    rejoice,
Go thou to Bethlehem, and see the child
  New born, beneath its mother's beaming
    smile, —
Look at thine own, and ponder there the while
It laughs, for life alone exulting wild!

That child, it has no memory of wrong;
  That child, it fears not coming days of woe;
  That child, it knows not that days come and go;
That child knows not that hours are short or
    long!
Better than thou to careworn, anxious men,
That careless child will preach the " to be born
    again."

ELI AND SAMUEL.

THE open vision ceases from the land,
  God's word becomes more rare, and yet more
      rare;
Eli, thine eyes wax dim! although thou stand
  In God's own house, thou dost not see him
      there!
He speaks! list, Eli, to the precious word!
  Alas, that word is not for such as thee;
Thy sealed ears no voice of God have heard, —
  Thy sluggard eyes no open vision see.
Wherefore should not the lamp of God burn
      out?
  The seer of God is blind, and nothing sees!
Who shall light Israel through her clouds of
      doubt?
  Whom shall God call upon in nights like
      these?
The priest dreams still of earth. Lo! God has
      smiled,
And called on one like heaven, — a ministering
      child.

HAGAR DEPARTED.

GENESIS XXI. 9–21.

A MOTHER drives a mother from her home!
   With tears the patriarch sees that dawning
      day;
With tears the child receives an outcast's
      doom;
   With tears his mother leads him far away!

The desert welcomes those by men outcast;
   The desert sees her want and hears her cry,
"Beneath this parched shade, rest, child, thy
      last!
   Let not thy mother see her darling die!"

Tears are but dew-drops at gray morning-tide,
   And God has beams of love to dry them
      all;
Deserts are wide, but his reign far more wide
   Who from the rock can bid the fountain fall.

"Hagar, arise! and bid thy boy arise!
   The orphan's God, the widow's helper, know!
Tears flow not vainly from a mother's eyes;
   See at thy feet the living waters flow!
The desert echoes not in vain his cries;
   God hears him in the agony of woe, —
   God shall be with him wheresoe'er he go!"

PALM SUNDAY AND EASTER.

A ROADWAY carpeted with palms and flowers,
  A welcome shouted by the eager throng;
  A thousand voices sing in David's song,
" Messiah comes, the nation's king and ours! "

Shouts, songs, and palms! Yet, as the week
      goes by
The shouts are silenced and the palms are dry,
Till that last day, when blackness shrouds the
      sky,
And those who shouted then to-day cry *Crucify!*

A cold, dark morning, and a new-made tomb;
Three weeping women groping through the
      gloom,
To dress a corpse from which the life has gone.
"And who shall roll away for us the stone!"
Only one streak of twilight, cold and gray,
Whitens the east and gives a hope of day;
But see, it mounts the heavens! "The Sun!
      the Sun!"
See for the world *Eternal Life* begun.

ON A YOUNG PREACHER.

[From an old Hymn-Book.]

PAUL, ere he preached, in lonely deserts strayed;
Far from his race for three long years he stayed.
If knowing nothing of mankind were all,
Our new-fledged preacher were a second Paul.

MARCH, 1841.

VI.

SONNETS, VALENTINES, BIRTHDAYS, ETC., AND SO FORTH.

Every one who is not a fool has written two sonnets.

Spanish proverb.

SONNETS, ETC.

IF Johnson, Whitney, and John Walker let
  The words flow freely which describe my lot,
  You shall discern what was and what was not,
That long-spun night I drank my Mocha late.
Alas, those heated grains inoculate
  My blood with fevered fancies of the cup,
  Because fair Chloe bade me drink it up!

Not so your fragrant draught of chocolate,
  Though all day long I saw your gracious
      smile,
  Which gave the cup with Aztec nectar filled,
  Dull brown below, all crowned with foamy
      white;
When day retired, and all men ceased from toil,
And sought sweet sleep and her refreshment
      mild,
  I forgot cup and all and slept all night!

"SEND ME!"

Not mine to mount to courts where seraphs
      sing,
Or glad archangels soar on outstretched wing;
Not mine in union with celestial choirs
To sound heaven's trump, or strike the gentler
      wires;
Not mine to stand enrolled at crystal gates,
Where Michael thunders or where Uriel waits.
But lesser worlds a Father's kindness know;
Be mine some simple service here below, —
To weep with those who weep, their joys to
      share,
Their pain to solace, or their burdens bear;
Some widow in her agony to meet;
Some exile in his new-found home to greet;
To serve some child of thine, and so serve thee, —
Lo, here am I! To such a work send me!

SONNET.

TO THE SHIP WHICH BROUGHT A COPY OF MICHAEL
ANGELO'S STATUE OF CHRIST FROM ITALY TO
AMERICA.

BARK after bark has sunk in gales like these,
Facing the jealous West, as thou dost now.
Still thou must breast each wave, nor shun the
seas,
Which beetle downward on thy westward prow.
The great "Christ-bearer" quailed not: he, as
thou,
Left Italy to seek our Western shore;
And, as another dove another olive bore,
Seeing across the waste another promise-bow.

Beat westward still! beat downward every wave!
The Christ who gave our New World to the Old,
E'en then his secret to his Michael told,
And to his eye the sacred vision gave.
Beat the waves down! let them his form behold
Who are his "other sheep," not of his early fold.

ANTIQUARIAN HALL, Worcester.

WHITE, BLUE, AND GREEN.

WHITE, blue, and green, — the whirling train
Flies through the hills, across the plain.
The varied landscape rushes by,
With wood and snow and distant sky;
And still the powers that shift the scene
Dress it in white and blue and green.

No scarlet of the tropic zone,
No purple of imperial rule;
The days of storm and blood are gone, —
This world is calm, serene, and cool.
White earth, blue sky, and spread between
Forests of living evergreen.

Ride on forever thus, in sooth,
In snow-white innocence of youth,
With heaven's own blue above the scene
Of life's eternal evergreen.

PROVIDENCE RAILWAY.

A VALENTINE.

My Lady, — Gold and silver rust,
And diamonds wear away to dust;
  These three alone eternal prove,
  In earth below and heaven above, —
  Faith, hope, and love.

This vase, by Benvenuto wrought,
  This coronal of gold,
These diamonds, from Golconda brought,
  Will tarnish and grow old.
Such gifts as these my lady's friend
In proof of friendship scorns to send;
  He sends what will eternal prove,
  Though rolling worlds forget to move, —
  A faithful servant's hopeful love.

ON THE TRAIN.

I.

[At the junction; on the tender-step.]

Bill. John, you 're here too early; see,
Here 's the schedule time.
Four full minutes here to wait,
Or we smash the downward freight!

John. Bill, I know it, and I try
To hold her back; she seems to fly!
Steam will make, and coal will burn,
Water boil, and drivers turn.
All ahead of time, — and I
And you know why!

II.

[At the drawbridge; on the tender-step, as before.]

Bill. All ahead of time again;
We shall smash the local train!
Thunder! John, the devil 's in it;
See the watch, — six, seven minute!

John. Don't you think I know it, Bill?
Do you think we have our will?
 She will go, and nothing hinders,
 Though the piston fly to flinders.
She will fly, — and you and I,
Bill, we know the reason why!

III.

[At the station.]

John. Nothing hinders, nothing blocks;
All ahead of cards and clocks!
 How the boss will swear, I know,
 When upstairs he hears her blow!
Good for boss, if he discover
Boss can't part a girl and lover.

See her standing at the door, —
See her run along the floor.
There! John baggage-man has found her;
See him throw his arms around her.
If you thought the boy would miss her,
See him catch her up and kiss her.
 Now the boss and you and I
 Know what makes the piston fly, —
  We know why!

ON THE AUTOCRAT'S EIGHTIETH BIRTHDAY.

HE taught me my geology;
    From him I knew
How, in their rabble rout,
    The crazy crew
    Of giants threw
Their pudding and their plums about.

He taught me modesty;
    In sitting at his feet
    I said that I
    Would never try
        To be
    As funny as is he.
And this, dear " Critic," will account for me.

And how to breakfast he
Has taught the world, — to be
Wise in such wise as Wisdom's self is wise;
    Yet playful, kind, and true;
    To mingle old and new,

And well the mixture brew;
　　With fittest reason
　　The bowl to season,
Then ladle out, profuse, for me and you.

　　But when the war-cloud growls and lowers
　　　Above the land,
　　　He takes command,
　　And shows the coward how to try,
　　And shows the bravest how to die;
Tyrtaeus sings, and cheers his boys and ours!

　　Blessings and thanks and praise,
　　In stumbling verse, in sweetest lays;
　　　And if grief come
　　Even to a prophet-poet's home,
To him some measure of the peace and faith,
The hope and strength which conquer death,
　　　Which, in our darker days,
　　With all a poet's prophecy,
　　And all a prophet's poetry,
　　And all a wise man's wisdom, he
　　Has sent to comfort you and me.

For the " Critic," August, 1889.
9

MY GOLD MINE.

[A poem which I will give to any one who will put it in rhyme.]

A SPANISH soldier passed this way,
    Hot, tired, wretched;
His head was bare, his feet were sore,
And his breast-plate and his morion hung
    Upon the beast he led.
He dipped up the sand with his hands,
He kicked it with his feet, —
And all the time he muttered,
    " Oro, oro, — Nada, — nada "
    " (Gold, gold, — there is no gold)."

Hot and tired, he sat under the pines,
    And from his haversack
He took his last Cuban orange, —
    This at least was golden.
    He sucked it dry,
And threw the skin and seeds away.

Then the Furies drove him forward,
And he tramped on, upon his way,
Bending his head down to look at the sand,
Kicking it with his feet, and grumbling as he
    walked,
  " Nada, nada, — Oro, oro "
  " (Gold, gold, — there is no gold)."

      I came this way
Three hundred years after him, and more;
I was not looking for gold, —
I knew there was no gold here.
      I was looking for the sky, and I found it.
I had escaped from my winter prison,
      Where the sky is gray;
Here I found a home for my bride
      Where the sky is blue.

Where the Spanish tramp had thrown away
The skin and seeds of his orange in the hummock,
There had grown a jungle of orange-trees.
      I cut off the fragrant flowers
      To take to my sweetheart,
To make a nosegay for our wedding
      In her frozen prison.

By the hummock I made my home,
And here I brought my bride,
    Away from her prison;
Here she lives with me, and here my children
    live, —
    We do not live in prison.

    I budded the orange-trees
With the shoots of other orange-blossoms,
Which my sweetheart brought from her prison.
    I screened them from the sun;
I hoed away the weeds from around the roots,
    And the buds grew,
And the trees grew, — you can see them, —
    There — and there — and there!

Stranger, eat the fruit,
    There is more than enough for all.
These are the true glories of the Hesperides;
    For these Alcides sailed;
These are the true apples of gold.

My boys pick all the fruit which no one eats;
    They send it North upon the rail,
To the poor wretches who live in the frozen
    prisons.

Stranger, here is the draft
Which those people in ice have sent for it.
Do you understand the writing, stranger?
I shall give it to my wife here.
It means that her golden fruit has brought her
    What the Spanish tramp did not find.
She is my Danae,
    And it will fill her lap with gold.

ORONADA, Soto County, Florida,
        April 1, 1891.

THE END.

**THIS BOOK IS DUE ON THE LAST DATE
STAMPED BELOW**

AN INITIAL FINE OF 25 CENTS

WILL BE ASSESSED FOR FAILURE TO RETURN
THIS BOOK ON THE DATE DUE. THE PENALTY
WILL INCREASE TO 50 CENTS ON THE FOURTH
DAY AND TO $1.00 ON THE SEVENTH DAY
OVERDUE.

JUL 25 1946	

M41947

THE UNIVERSITY OF CALIFORNIA LIBRARY

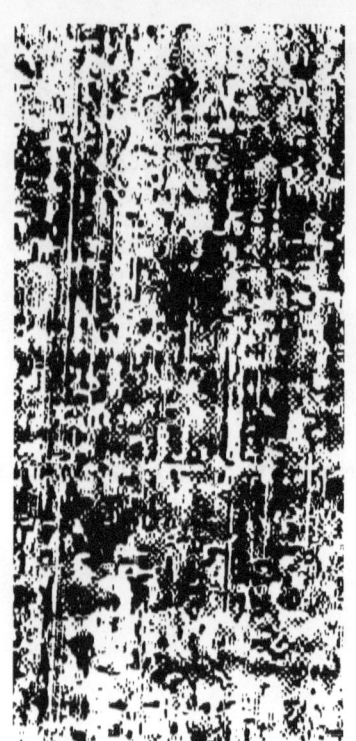

www.ingramcontent.com/pod-product-compliance
Lightning Source LLC
Chambersburg PA
CBHW021136020726
47500CB00003B/1114